·M·O·R·E·
BALLOON ANIMALS

AARON HSU-FLANDERS

CB
CONTEMPORARY BOOKS

Library of Congress Cataloging-in-Publication Data

Hsu-Flanders, Aaron.
    More balloon animals / Aaron Hsu-Flanders.
       p.   cm.
    ISBN 0-8092-4183-8
    1. Balloon sculpture.   I. Title.
  TT926.H785   1990
  745.594—dc20
                    89-49334
                      CIP

Line drawings by Lillian Hsu-Flanders
Photos copyright © 1989 by David Caras

Published by Contemporary Books
An imprint of NTC/Contemporary Publishing Company
4255 West Touhy Avenue, Lincolnwood (Chicago), Illinois 60646-1975 U.S.A.
Copyright © 1990 by Aaron Hsu-Flanders
Printed in the United States of America
International Standard Book Number: 0-8092-4183-8

28   27   26   25   24   23   22   21   20   19   18   17   16   15   14   13

This book is for
Lily Yung Sing
and Adriel Shao Ling.

ACKNOWLEDGMENTS

Profuse thanks to Lillian Hsu-Flanders, Adriel Hsu-Flanders, Richard Argosh, Dr. Ivan Ciric, David Caras, Harvey Plotnick, Georgene Sainati, Cathy Mahar, Stacy Prince, Joe Skutas, Jeff Hunter, Eric Persson, Alexander Feldman, City Stage Co., and everyone at Contemporary Books. You have all enabled me to write this book, in one way or another.

CAUTION:

Do *not* put inflated, tied balloons in your mouth for any reason. Even if you wish you had a few extra hands to make a certain animal, resist the temptation to hold a balloon part between your lips even for a second; if the balloon pops you could have a piece of latex forced down your throat. For this reason it is best not to let children under the age of three—who cannot help putting everything in their mouths—handle the balloons at all. Even uninflated balloons can cause choking or suffocation. Be sure to supervise any child under the age of seven who wishes to make balloon animals himself or herself.

CONTENTS

·M·O·R·E·
BALLOON
ANIMALS

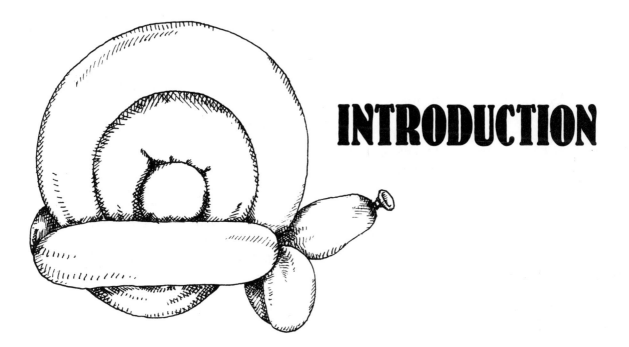

INTRODUCTION

Balloon animals are here to stay! When my first book, *Balloon Animals*, came out, even I was surprised at the level of excitement it generated. All authors think they have a "bestseller"; I was thrilled to find out I really did! It was also gratifying to receive letters from children and adults all over the world. Because the number of readers wanting instructions for more animals was so large, I got out my typewriter once again and banged out instructions for 20 more popular balloon creatures, many of them my personal favorites. I told you this was fun!

More Balloon Animals is designed to be rewarding even for novice balloon sculptors, so please don't worry if you haven't read *Balloon Animals* yet. But please be aware that I have presented these new animals in order of difficulty. For that reason I suggest that if this is your first experience making balloon animals you start from the beginning of the book. There is important information on how to inflate, tie, and handle balloons in the beginning pages. Certain crucial points are explained in depth in "Beginner Balloon Animals," and if you jump

too far ahead you might get a little confused. And when you actually begin making each animal, be sure to read all of the instructions before you start. That way you will know what to expect and your hands won't be tied up in knots when you need to turn a page.

This book comes with 20 balloons, but don't be surprised if you're not a professional balloon artist by the time your balloons run out. You'll get much better with a little practice, and believe me, once you start making balloon animals for your friends— especially your little ones—

you'll get a lot of practice! If you want to buy more of these balloons in a store, I suggest trying your local novelty, joke, or magic shop. In case you cannot find them anywhere, or would rather order them by mail, I have included a few mail-order sources in the back of the book. Be sure to ask for the #260 variety of balloons.

I hope that you find this book as amusing and interesting to use as it was for me to writc. Whether you are twisting balloon animals for the pure pleasure of making yourself or others happy, or you intend to make a little extra money performing, I think these animals will fill the bill. I wish you many years of inflated-balloon fun and twisted-balloon pleasure.

BEFORE YOU START

A FEW REMARKS ABOUT THE BALLOONS

Always keep your balloons in a cool, dry place. This will keep them fresh for a few months. And try to avoid twisting balloon animals in direct sunlight, as heat makes the balloons more susceptible to popping. I would also suggest keeping your fingernails smooth and well rounded and removing any jewelry (such as rings or bracelets that could accidentally puncture a balloon) before you begin.

After you've inflated and tied a balloon (directions for inflating and tying are in the next section), you'll want to be sure to keep it away from sharp objects. You should also avoid running your hands up and down the sides of the balloon, as this can weaken it and cause it to pop.

Always begin twisting your balloon at the end where it is tied, working toward the uninflated end. This will allow the air in the balloon to move downward toward the tail as you make your twists. Be careful to hold the balloon as shown in the photos, whether you are right- or left-handed, as it will make the directions simpler to follow. It is also important to remember to give smaller bubbles a few extra twists; the smaller the bubble, the more twists you need to secure it. Of course, before you know it, you'll have a feel for the balloons, and all these tips will be second nature.

Remember that these balloons are not all exactly the same size. For this reason some of your animals might end up looking a little different from the ones in the photos. This is fine. Your animals don't need to look exactly like mine to be wonderfully perfect. It's okay if your pig has a little longer snout than the one in the book. All balloon artists make their own versions of these animals, and even professionals must vary proportions to fit each balloon. A good rule of thumb is to keep the proportions right rather than try to measure the bubbles. So if you begin to run out of tail section as you are making your animal, make the rest of your bubbles a little smaller than usual. If you have too much tail section as you are making your animal, make the remaining bubbles a little bigger. Experiment. If it isn't working out, untwist your balloon and begin again. If you keep having trouble, double-check the length of the tail you leave when you inflate the balloon; it is the most important measurement to take for each animal.

There is no such thing as a bad balloon animal. If you are trying to make a cat and you finish to find your creation doesn't look anything like a cat, then you have simply made a new balloon animal. Sometimes balloon animals are actually invented this way; some of the best animals have grown out of "mistakes." Almost anything you come up with is bound to look adorable.

These balloons are made specifically for twisting. In fact, they are not used for anything *except* twisting. They are stronger than regular balloons. Because of this, you needn't be afraid to turn them, stretch them, or do anything that the instructions tell you to do to them. Occasionally, however, balloons do pop, often without apparent reason. It is wise, therefore, to avoid twisting balloon animals in a place where a sudden, loud, popping noise would be disturbing.

I don't advise drawing on these balloons, as it increases the chances that the balloons will pop. If you can't resist, please use a felt-tip marker.

Reminder: DON'T put inflated, tied balloons in your mouth.

INFLATING THE BALLOON

I recommend using the small hand pump included in this kit. Balloons are difficult to inflate with your own lungs, and the pump works quite well. Using the pump will also allow you to make as many balloon animals as you want, without getting tired from inflating them. Here are a few suggestions for inflating the balloons:

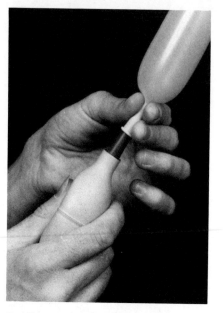

the balloon about 1 inch over the nozzle. Hold it in place with the thumb and index finger of one hand. With your other hand, slowly begin inflating the balloon by squeezing and releasing the bulb of the pump.

1. Stretch the balloon lengthwise a few times before you inflate it. Slip the end of the balloon over the nozzle of the pump. Roll the neck of

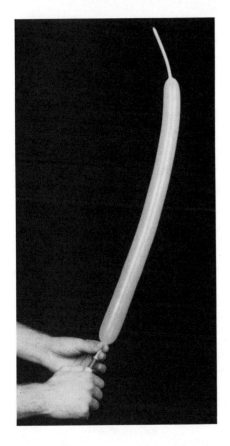

2. Fill the balloon until there is an appropriate length of tail on the end. Each animal requires a specific amount of tail, which allows the air in the balloon to expand as you make your twists.

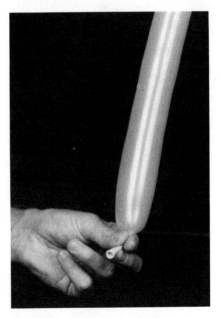

3. Slip the neck of the balloon off the nozzle of the pump, but continue pinching the neck of the balloon to keep the air inside.

TYING THE BALLOON

There are many good ways to tie a balloon. Any way that works for you is fine. These are the steps that I follow:

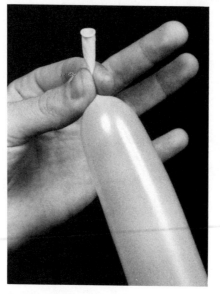

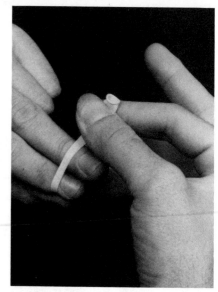

1. Let a tiny bit of air out of the balloon so that the neck of the balloon is a little longer and more flexible. Hold the neck of the balloon between your thumb and index finger.

2. Stretch the neck of the balloon over the backs of your index and middle fingers.

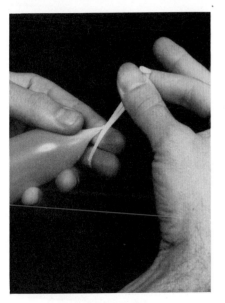 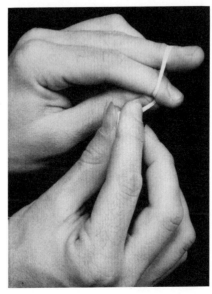 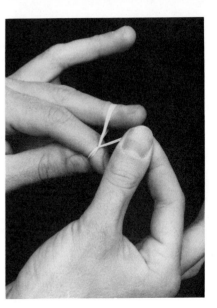

3. Continue stretching the neck of the balloon around the fronts of your index and middle fingers.

4. Separate your index and middle fingers to create a small space.

5. Push the neck of the balloon through this space.

6. Holding the neck of the balloon, slide the rest of the balloon off your index and middle fingers.

7. Give a little tug and you have your knot.

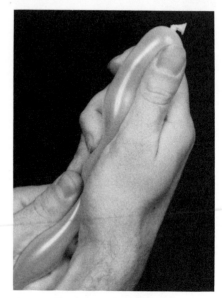

8. Before you begin twisting any of the animals in this book, squeeze each balloon gently at the knot end to lessen the tension in the balloon.

12

BEGINNER
BALLOON ANIMALS

ANTEATER

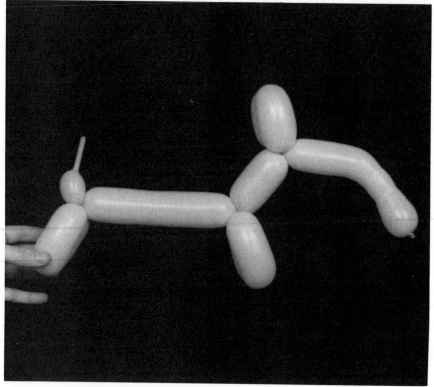

The anteater always gets a good laugh. Until someone invents a balloon ant, I would feed your anteater air!

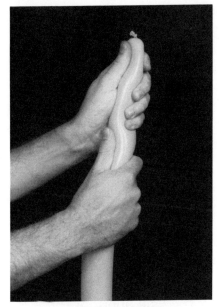

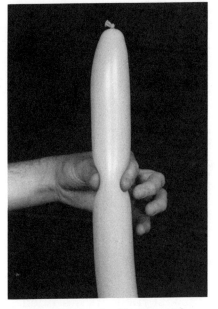

1. Begin by inflating a balloon and leaving a 4-inch tail on the end. Tie a knot.

2. Squeeze the balloon gently below the knot to lessen the tension in the balloon and to make the snout of the anteater more pliable.

3. Pinch the balloon with the thumb and index finger of one hand, about 6 inches from the knot.

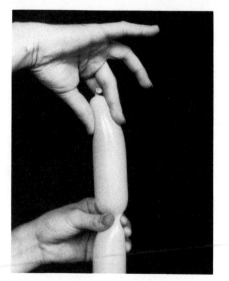 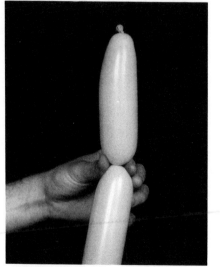 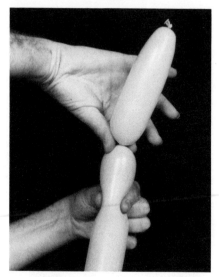

4. With your free hand, twist the 6-inch section of balloon around, two full turns, away from your body.

5. This bubble will form the long snout of the anteater. Hold on to this twist gently with the thumb and index finger of one hand. This prevents it from untwisting.

6. While you're holding this twist, pinch off a 2-inch bubble directly below the first 6-inch bubble.

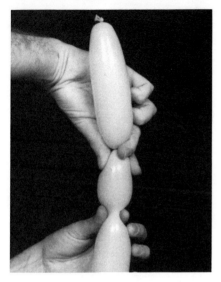 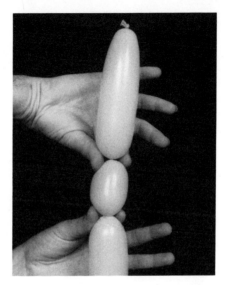 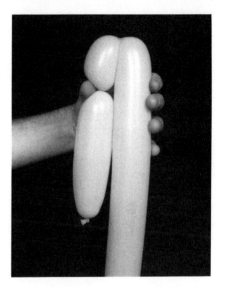

7. Twist the balloon
around a couple of times
at this new point.

8. You will now be holding
on to both twists so that
they don't untwist.

9. Fold the 6-inch bubble
and the 2-inch bubble
down alongside the
remaining length of
balloon.

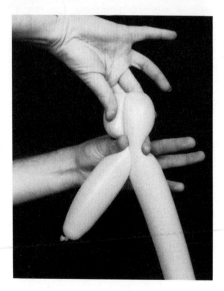

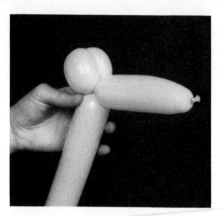

10. Pinch the remaining length of balloon at the point where the first twist meets it. You will notice that this creates a second 2-inch bubble.

11. Twist the two 2-inch bubbles, rotating them together, about two full turns.

12. This rotating locks your previous twists in place, forming the snout and ears of your anteater. This last twist will be used again and again throughout this book. It will be referred to as the *locking twist.* Now your hands are free to make the rest of your anteater.

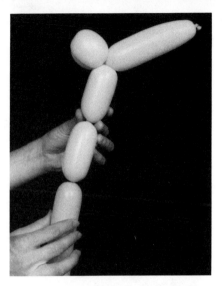 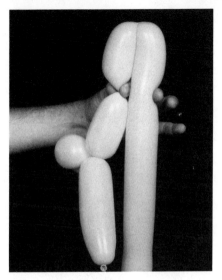 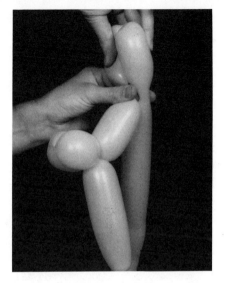

13. Pinch off and twist two 3-inch bubbles below the snout and ears section of your anteater. Hold on to these twists so they don't untwist.

14. Fold these two bubbles down alongside the remaining length of balloon and pinch the remaining length of balloon where it meets the twist between the two 3-inch bubbles.

15. Join these bubbles with a locking twist.

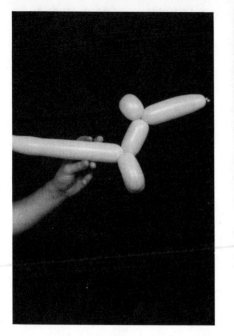

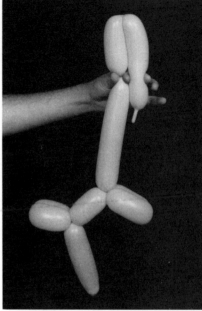

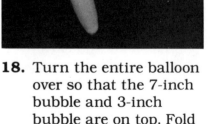

16. This will form the neck
and front legs of your
anteater.

17. Now pinch off and twist
a 7-inch bubble and a
3-inch bubble. Hold on
to both twists so they
don't untwist.

18. Turn the entire balloon
over so that the 7-inch
bubble and 3-inch
bubble are on top. Fold
the remaining length of

balloon over so that it meets the twist between the 7-inch and 3-inch bubbles. Pinch the remaining length of balloon at this point.

19. Join these bubbles with a locking twist, leaving a little bubble on the end of the balloon for a tail.

20. Return to the snout of your anteater and gently tug on the knot while firmly squeezing the snout with your other hand. This will allow the balloon to expand a little and will make the snout more flexible.

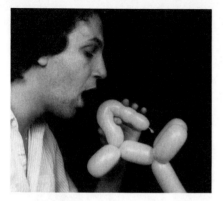 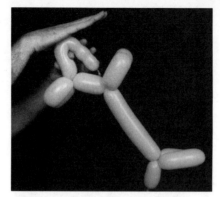 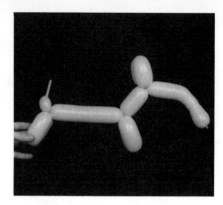

21. Fold the snout in half and breathe a little warm air from your mouth onto the folded section.

22. You may also rub the folded section lightly with your hand. This will help bend the nose into the shape of an anteater's snout.

23. This is the completed anteater.

CROCODILE

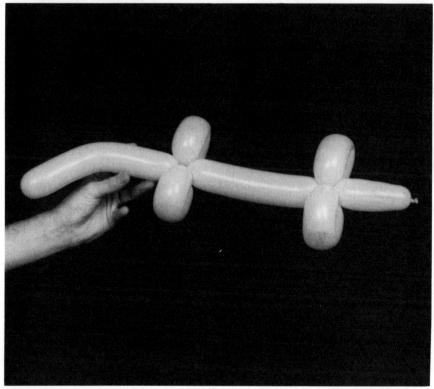

I've had a million requests for this animal. This one will also pass as an alligator!

 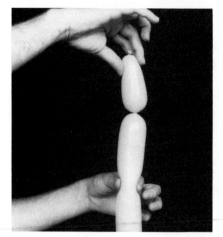 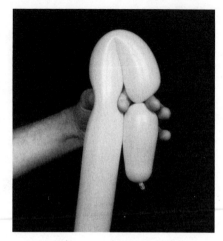

1. Inflate a balloon, leaving a 4-inch tail on the end, and tie a knot. Pinch the balloon about 3 inches below the knot and twist the balloon around a couple of times at this point. Hold on to this twist with one hand so that it doesn't untwist.

2. While holding on to this twist with one hand, pinch the balloon again, about 4 inches below the first twist.

3. Fold this 4-inch section in half so that the pinch you are holding meets the first twist you made.

24

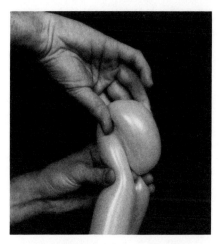

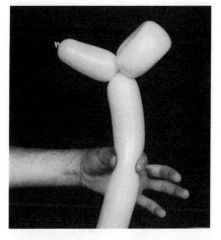

4. Twist the (folded) 4-inch bubble around a couple of times.

5. This will lock it in place, and you no longer need to hold on to it.

6. Pinch off a 4-inch bubble below the one you just made.

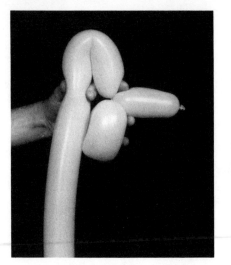 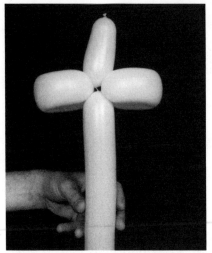 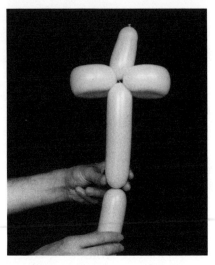

7. Fold it in half so that the pinch you are holding meets the same twist as before. Twist this 4-inch bubble around a couple of times.

8. This will lock it in place. You have just created the snout and two front legs of your crocodile. This is what it looks like so far.

9. Now pinch off a 5-inch bubble below the two front legs and twist the balloon around at this point. Hold on to your twist so that it doesn't untwist. This bubble will be the body of your crocodile.

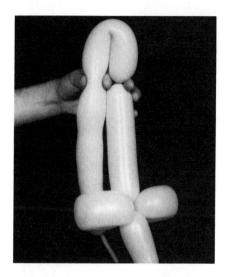

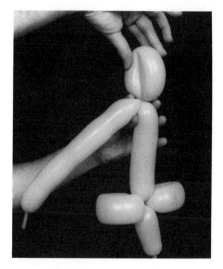

10. While holding that twist with one hand, pinch off another 4-inch bubble below the twist. This 4-inch bubble will be one of the back legs of your crocodile.

11. Fold this 4-inch bubble in half so that the pinch you are holding meets the twist at the end of the body section.

12. Twist the 4-inch bubble around a couple of times at this point. This will lock the body section and the first of the two back legs.

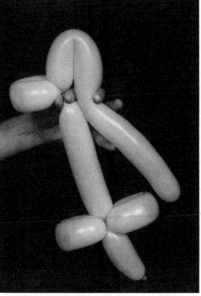
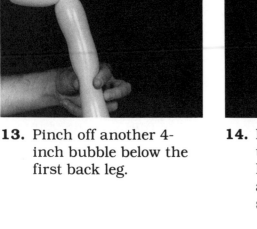
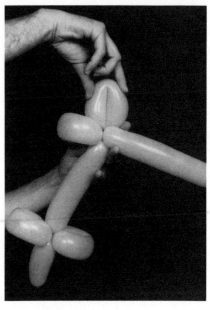

13. Pinch off another 4-inch bubble below the first back leg.

14. Fold it in half so that the pinch you are holding meets the twist at the end of the body section.

15. Twist the 4-inch bubble around a couple of times, as you have done for the other legs, to lock it in place.

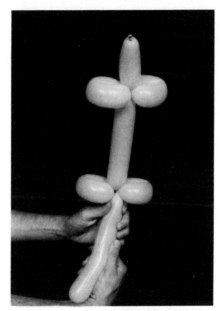

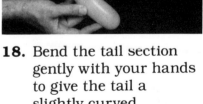

16. This is what your crocodile looks like so far.

17. Squeeze the last section of the balloon, which will be your crocodile's long tail, so that the air expands into and fills the entire tail section.

18. Bend the tail section gently with your hands to give the tail a slightly curved appearance.

19. This is the completed crocodile.

COCKER SPANIEL

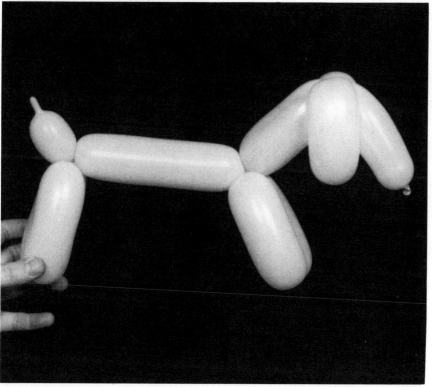

This is an adorable variation of the standard balloon dog.

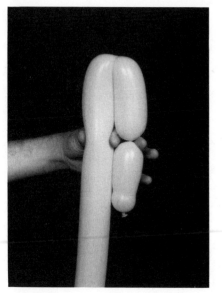

length of balloon. Pinch the remaining length of balloon where it meets the twist between the 4-inch and 3-inch bubbles.

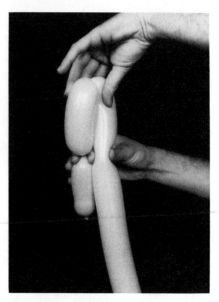

1. Inflate a balloon, leaving a 4-inch tail on the end, and tie a knot. Make a 3-inch bubble, followed by a 4-inch bubble, and fold both bubbles down alongside the remaining

2. Join these three bubbles with a locking twist. This forms the nose and ears of your cocker spaniel.

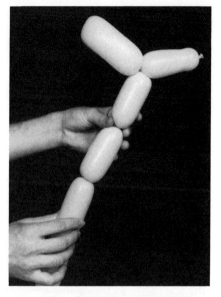 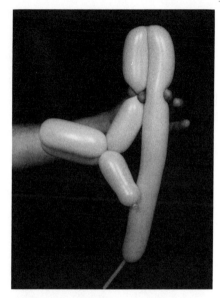 

3. Make a 4-inch bubble for the neck and a 4-inch bubble for one of the front legs.

4. Fold these two bubbles down alongside the remaining length of balloon. Pinch the remaining balloon at the point where it meets the twist.

5. Join the bubbles with a locking twist. This will form both of the front legs as well as the neck.

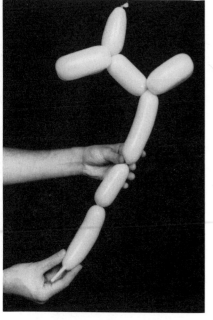

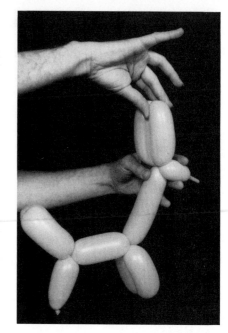

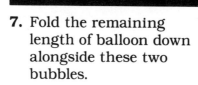

6. Make a 5-inch bubble for the body and a 4-inch bubble for one of the back legs.

7. Fold the remaining length of balloon down alongside these two bubbles.

8. Join the bubbles with a locking twist. This will form the back legs and the body of your cocker spaniel.

  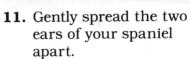

9. This is what your cocker spaniel looks like so far.

10. Now twist the ears of your cocker spaniel over so that they are upside down.

11. Gently spread the two ears of your spaniel apart.

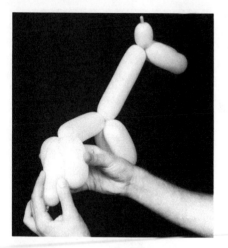

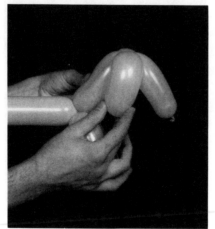

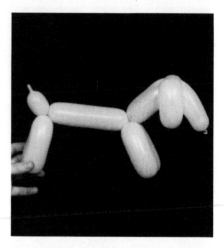

12. Gently push the base of the spaniel's nose between the two spread ears so that it is wedged between the ears.

13. Do the same thing with the neck of the spaniel, behind the two spread ears. This might take a little practice, because it feels a little weird, but it is really not that difficult. Keep playing with the positioning until it looks right.

14. This is the completed cocker spaniel.

HUMMINGBIRD

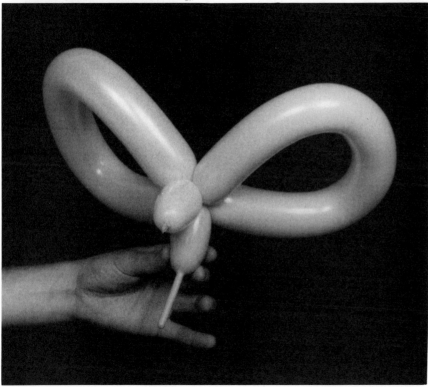

This is an easy creation and a favorite of children of all ages.

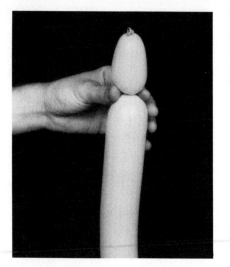 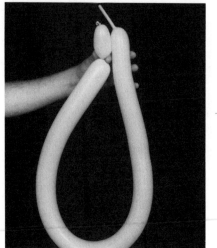 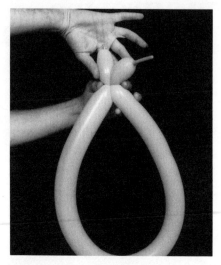

1. Inflate a balloon, leaving a 2-inch tail on the end, and tie a knot. Make a 2-inch bubble below the knot and hold on to it.

2. Bring the 2-inch bubble all the way around to the tail end of the balloon and line it up so that it is even with the inflated part of the tail end.

3. Pinch the tail end to form a 2-inch bubble on the tail end. Then join these two bubbles with a locking twist. You should now have a large balloon loop. Hold the loop so that the 2-inch bubbles are at the top.

 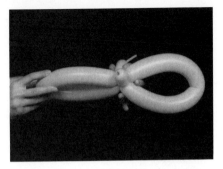 

4. Bring the 2-inch bubbles down until they meet the balloon loop at the opposite side of the loop. This will split the balloon loop in half and form two wings for your hummingbird.

5. Turn one of the wings around a couple of times to lock the wings in place.

6. This is what your hummingbird looks like at this point.

inside one of the wings and spread them apart. Then press the index finger of your other hand on the outside of the wing, toward the space between your spread fingers. Press down gently but firmly.

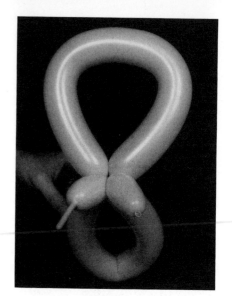

7. To make your wings a little more hummingbirdlike, put a thumb and a finger

8. This is what one hummingbird wing looks like. Repeat this process for the other wing.

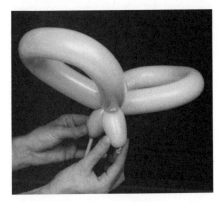 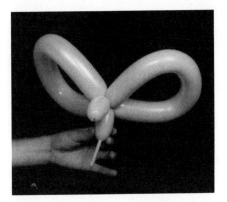

9. Adjust the 2-inch bubbles so that they are both below the hummingbird's wings.

10. This is the completed hummingbird.

41

FISH

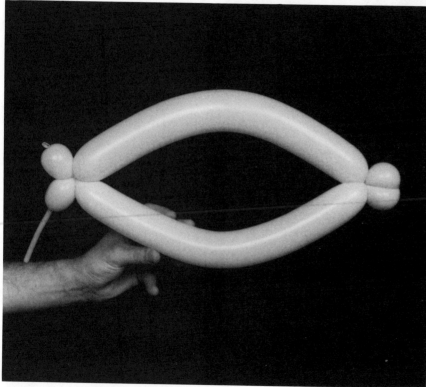

The fish is simple to make
and has a nice, sleek look.

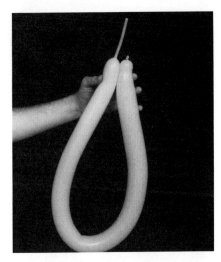 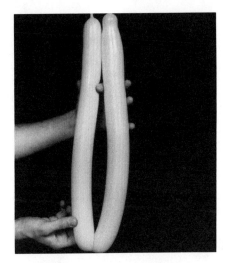 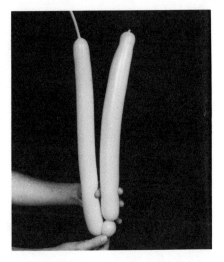

1. Inflate a balloon, leaving a 3-inch tail on the end, and tie a knot. Squeeze the balloon well, below the knot, to lessen the tension in the balloon. Fold the balloon in half, lining up the knot end and the tail end.

2. Make a twist in the balloon at the midpoint, dividing the balloon in half.

3. Make a 1-inch bubble to one side of the twist and hold on to it so it doesn't untwist.

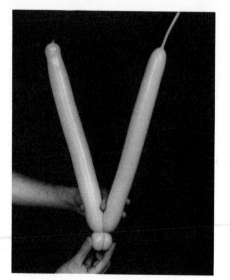

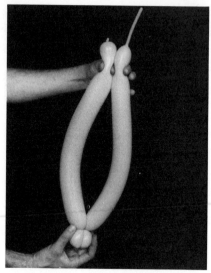

4. Do the same thing on the other side of the twist so that you have two 1-inch bubbles in the middle of the balloon.

5. Twist these two bubbles around each other so that they lock. Then twist them around a few extra times. This isn't a typical locking twist, so it needs more twists to stay secure.

6. Return to the knot and tail ends of your balloon and line them up again. Pinch off about 1 inch of each end.

9. This is the completed fish.

7. Twist the two bubbles formed by your pinches around each other a couple of times so that they lock.

8. Stretch the two long sections of your fish so that the body is more rounded.

DUCK

This animal is an interesting variation of the standard swan (which I included in my first book, *Balloon Animals*). It will make bath time extra fun.

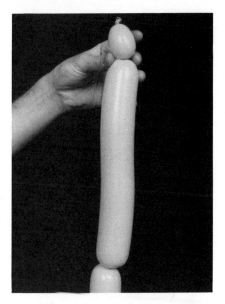 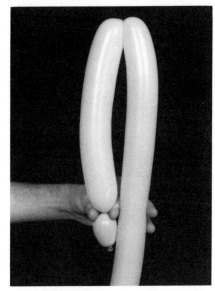 

1. Inflate a balloon, leaving a 3-inch tail on the end, and tie a knot. Make a 1-inch bubble and a 12-inch bubble. Hold on to both of these bubbles so they don't untwist.

2. Fold both of these bubbles down alongside the length of balloon.

3. Join the bubbles with a locking twist.

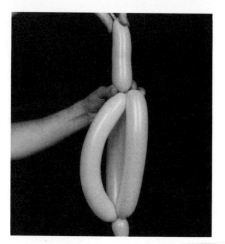  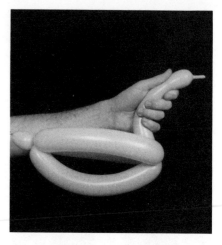

4. Fold the remaining length of balloon over so that it lies between the two 12-inch bubbles. Pinch the remaining length of balloon where it meets the twist between the two 12-inch bubbles, and make a twist at this point.

5. Wrap the entire tail end around the twist between the two 12-inch bubbles. You will actually pass it through the two 12-inch bubbles so that it locks.

6. Gently squeeze the tail section of the balloon (which is the head of your duck) so that the air in it expands and almost fills it.

9. This is the completed duck.

7. Fold this bubble in half and gently rub the fold with the palm of your hand. (You might also blow a little warm air onto the fold.) This will help bend the duck's neck.

8. Separate the two 12-inch bubbles with one hand and wedge the duck's neck firmly between the two 12-inch bubbles so that it is pointing upward. The end of the duck's neck—the duck's head—will be pointing slightly forward.

TURTLE

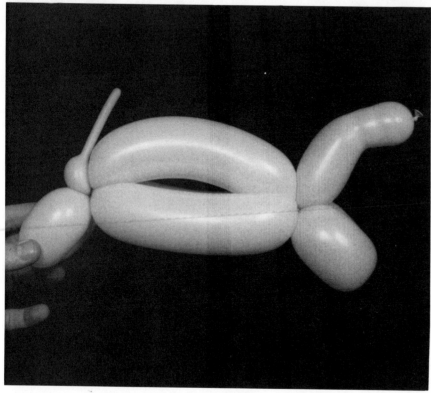

When I was growing up, almost all my friends had turtles. Now you can give a turtle to each of *your* friends.

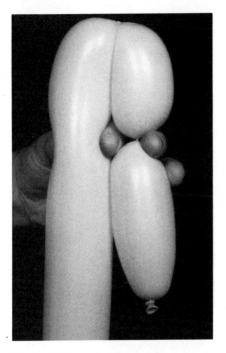

the knot, to lessen the tension. Make a 3-inch bubble, then a 2-inch bubble, and fold both bubbles down alongside the remaining length of balloon.

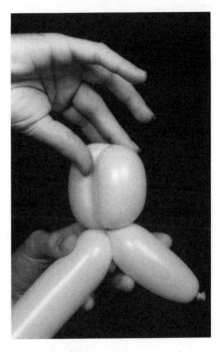

1. Inflate a balloon, leaving a 5-inch tail on the end, and tie a knot. Squeeze the balloon well, below

2. Join the bubbles with a locking twist. You now have the head and front legs of your turtle.

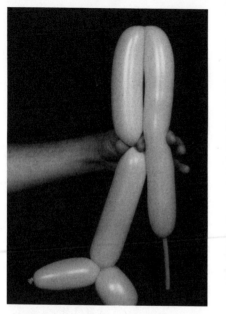 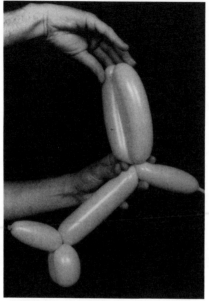 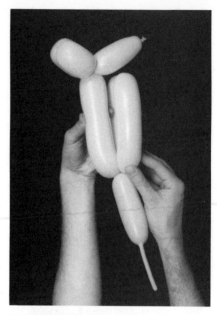

3. Make two 6-inch bubbles and fold them down alongside the remaining length of balloon.

4. Join the bubbles with a locking twist.

5. Lay the first 6-inch bubble between the two side-by-side 6-inch bubbles.

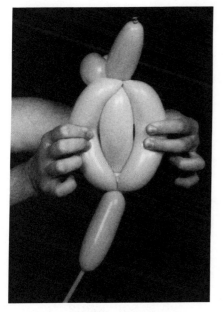 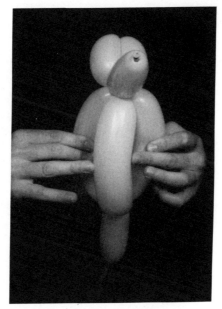 

6. Next, gently spread the two 6-inch bubbles apart and slowly begin to roll them around the first 6-inch bubble. Be careful not to force them.

7. Roll the second two bubbles all the way around the first 6-inch bubble until the first bubble is all the way through the second two.

8. This is what your turtle will look like at this point.

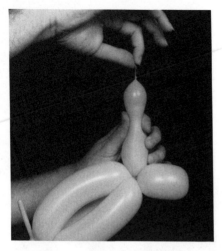

9. Make a 2-inch bubble with the remaining section of balloon and fold it down alongside the tiny section that is left after that.

10. Join these two bubbles with a locking twist, leaving a little balloon at the end for the tail. This will form the back legs of your turtle.

11. Return to the knot end of the balloon and gently tug on the knot while squeezing the 3-inch bubble that the knot is connected to. This gives you a little extra balloon at the knot and makes that bubble more flexible.

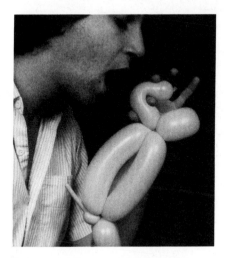

14. This is the completed turtle.

12. Now fold that 3-inch bubble in half and gently rub the outside of the fold with your hand. This will bend the head section of your turtle.

13. It helps to breathe a little warm air from your mouth onto the folded section too.

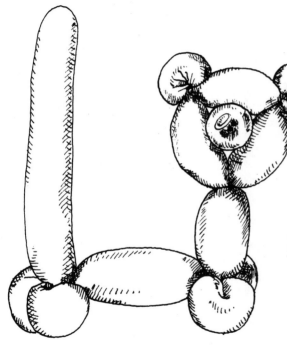

INTERMEDIATE
BALLOON ANIMALS

PARROT IN A SWING

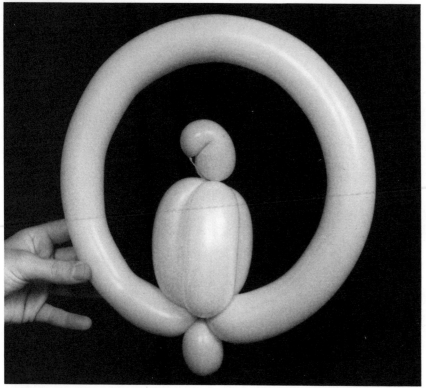

This is a very romantic balloon animal and one of the all-time classics.

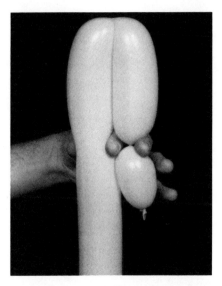 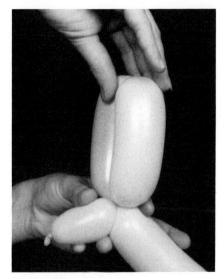 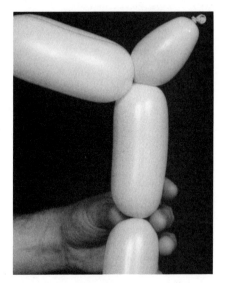

1. Inflate a balloon, leaving a 2-inch tail on the end, and tie a knot. Make a 2-inch bubble, then a 4-inch bubble, and fold both bubbles down alongside the remaining length of balloon.

2. Join the bubbles with a locking twist.

3. Make another 4-inch bubble just below the other two.

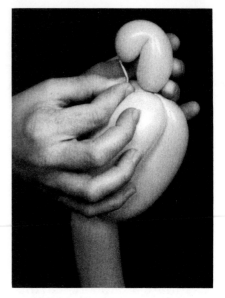

4. Gently roll the first two 4-inch bubbles around the third one.

5. Continue rolling the two 4-inch bubbles around the third until the third is all the way through the first two.

6. Grasp the knot on the 2-inch bubble and pull it down to the bottom of the 2-inch bubble.

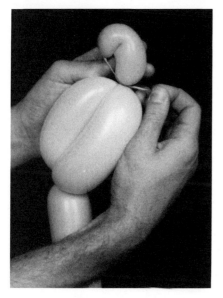  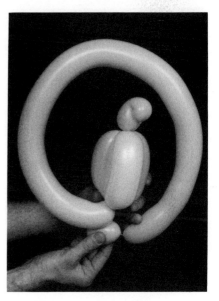

7. Wrap the knot around the twist at the bottom of the 2-inch bubble a few times until it stays in place by itself. This creates the parrot's sharp beak.

8. Make a 1-inch bubble at the tail end of the balloon.

9. While holding the 1-inch bubble, wrap the entire tail section of the balloon in an arc back around to the twist underneath the 4-inch bubbles.

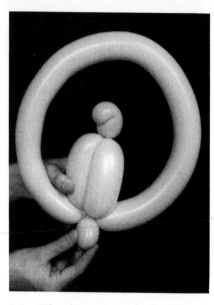

10. Wrap the 1-inch bubble around the twist underneath the 4-inch bubbles. You need only wrap it once; it will stay in place.

11. The last 1-inch bubble serves as your parrot's tail. This is the completed parrot in a swing.

DINOSAUR

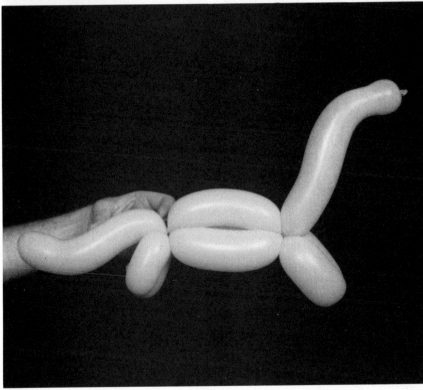

The dinosaur has been by far the most popular animal among kids for the past decade. Here is a balloon version designed by Eric "Cheezo" Persson.

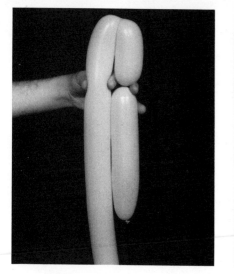

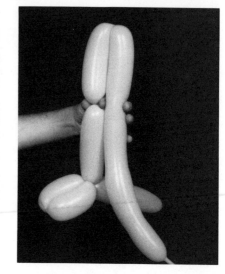

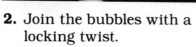

1. Inflate a balloon, leaving a 3-inch tail on the end, and tie a knot. Make a 7-inch bubble, then a 3-inch bubble, and fold both bubbles down alongside the remaining length of balloon.

2. Join the bubbles with a locking twist.

3. Make two 4-inch bubbles and fold them down alongside the remaining length of balloon.

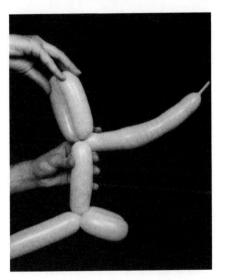

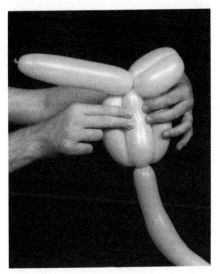

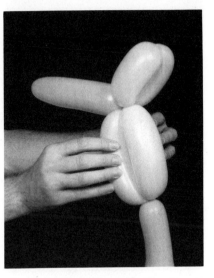

4. Now join these bubbles with a locking twist.

5. Gently spread the second two 4-inch bubbles and begin to roll them around the first 4-inch bubble.

6. Continue to roll the two bubbles all the way around the first until the first bubble passes through the second two.

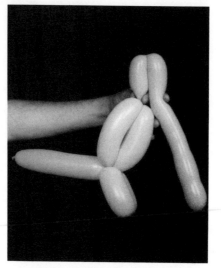

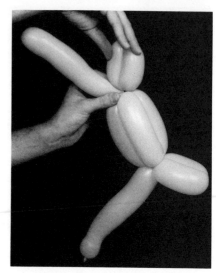

7. With the remaining length of balloon, make one 3-inch bubble.

8. Fold this bubble down alongside the remaining length of balloon.

9. Join the bubbles with a locking twist at the twist that already exists at the back of the last three 4-inch bubbles.

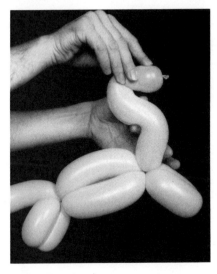

when the dinosaur is standing.

10. Bend the neck of the dinosaur, the 7-inch bubble you made first, so that it is curved. Gently rub the fold in the neck. Breathe a little warm air onto the fold to help shape it. (If you want, you can also pull on the knot to give you a little extra balloon.)

11. Do the same for the dinosaur's tail so it drags along the ground

12. Above is the completed dinosaur.

CAMEL

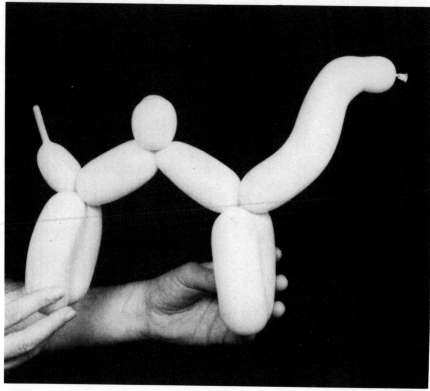

People have told me this animal is easy once you get over the hump!

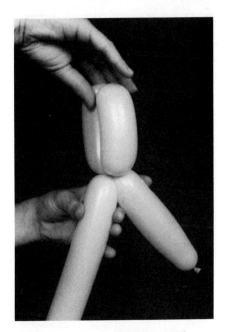

bubble for one of the front legs, and fold both bubbles down alongside the remaining length of balloon.

1. Inflate a balloon, leaving a 4-inch tail on the end, and tie a knot. Make a 6-inch bubble for the head and neck, then a 4-inch

2. Join the bubbles with a locking twist.

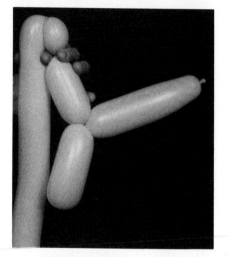 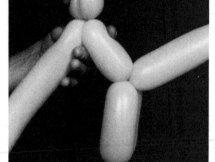 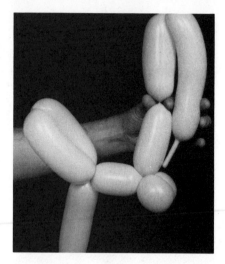

3. Make a 3-inch bubble, then a 1-inch bubble, and fold both bubbles down alongside the remaining length of balloon.

4. Join the bubbles with a locking twist at the point where you made the 1-inch bubble.

5. Make another 3-inch bubble, then a 4-inch bubble, and fold both bubbles down alongside the remaining length of balloon.

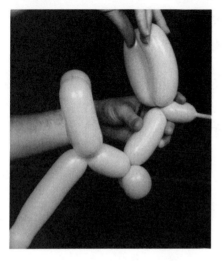 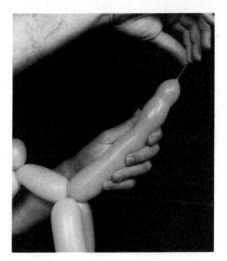 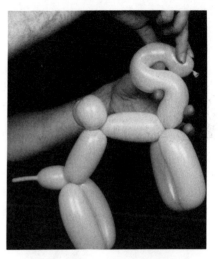

6. Join these with a locking twist, leaving a little bubble at the end for a tail.

7. Give a little tug on the knot while squeezing the long bubble gently with your hands. This will give you a little extra balloon at the knot end and will give your camel's head a nice shape.

8. Fold this long bubble into an *S* shape. Breathe a little warm air onto the folded parts of the camel's neck to curve it a little.

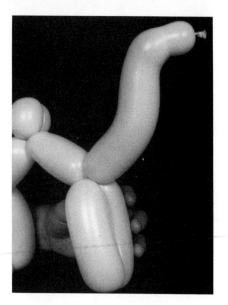

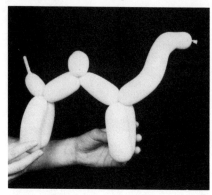

10. Position the hump on the camel's back sideways, if necessary, and you've got the completed camel.

9. When you let go of the camel's neck, it should hold some of its curve. If it does not, try folding it up again and rubbing the folded sections.

PIG/HIPPOPOTAMUS

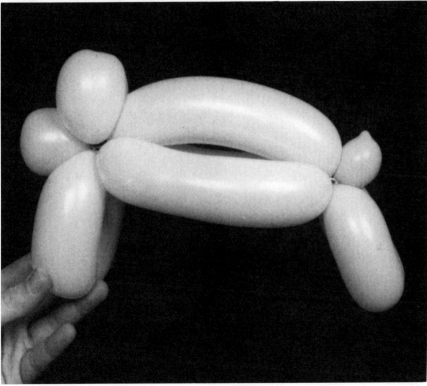

I can't stop chuckling when I look at this pig. It's squat and adorable. The hippo is one of my favorite inventions. It's an unusual but very appealing animal, and it's not that difficult to make—it's basically a pig with a longer snout and a neck!

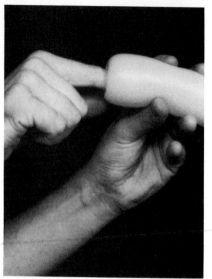

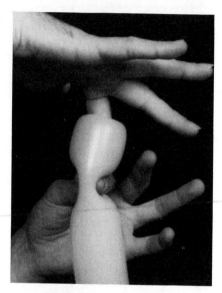

finger directly on the knot and press the knot about 2 inches into the balloon.

PIG

1. Inflate a balloon, leaving a 4-inch tail on the end, and tie a knot. Squeeze the balloon well, below the knot, to lessen the tension. Put your index

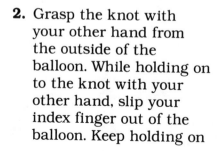

2. Grasp the knot with your other hand from the outside of the balloon. While holding on to the knot with your other hand, slip your index finger out of the balloon. Keep holding on

to the knot from the outside of the balloon. You'll notice you've pinched off a 2-inch bubble at this end.

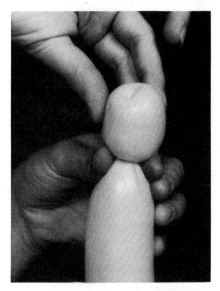

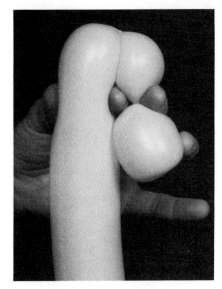

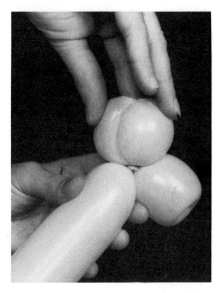

3. Still holding on to the knot, twist this bubble around a few times to lock the stem of the knot inside the balloon.

4. Make a 1-inch bubble below the 2-inch bubble that has the knot locked inside and fold both bubbles down alongside the remaining length of balloon.

5. Join these two small bubbles with a locking twist. You have now formed the snout and ears of your pig.

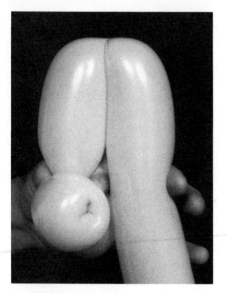 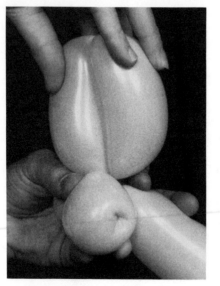 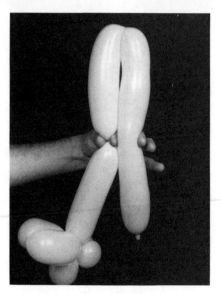

6. With the snout and ears locked in place, make a 3-inch bubble and fold it down alongside the remaining length of balloon.

7. Join the bubbles with a locking twist at the same point at which you joined the snout and ears. You have now formed the front legs of your pig.

8. Make two 6-inch bubbles and fold them down alongside the remaining length of balloon.

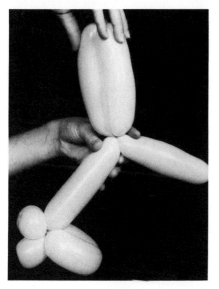  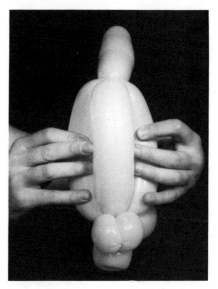

9. Join the bubbles with a locking twist.

10. Gently spread the second two 6-inch bubbles and begin to roll them around the first 6-inch bubble.

11. Roll the two bubbles all the way around the first 6-inch bubble. This will lock all three of the 6-inch bubbles and form the body of your pig.

bubble on the very end
for the pig's tail.

14. Above is the completed
pig.

12. Make a 3-inch bubble
and fold it down
alongside the
remaining length of
balloon.

13. Join the bubbles with a
locking twist at the
same point where the
three 6-inch bubbles
meet. This forms the
back legs of your pig.
Be sure to leave a little

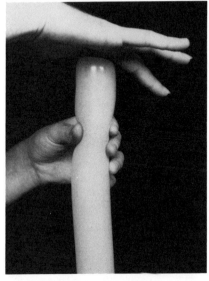

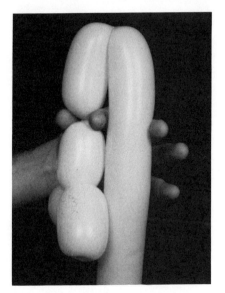

HIPPOPOTAMUS

1. Begin by following steps 1–3 for the pig, but push the knot *as far back* into the balloon as it will go to make the longer hippo snout.

2. Now follow steps 4–5 for the pig to create the hippo's nose and ears.

3. Make a 2-inch bubble for the neck and a 3-inch bubble for one of the front legs and fold them both down alongside the remaining length of balloon.

4. Join the bubbles with a locking twist.

5. Now follow steps 8–13 for the pig, but make the body bubbles 5 inches long. Here's your hippopotamus.

SNAIL

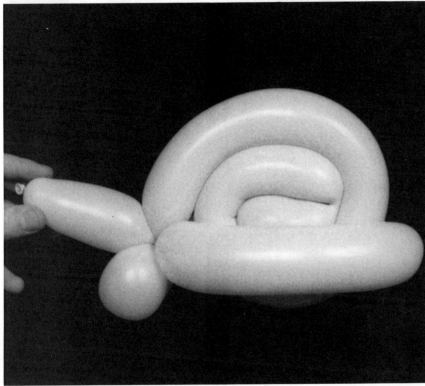

This is a fabulous balloon animal, and although people don't think to ask for it, they all love it when they see it.

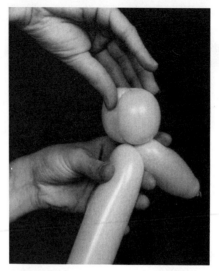

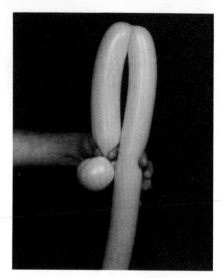

1. Inflate a balloon, leaving a 3-inch tail on the end, and tie a knot. Make a 3-inch bubble, then a 1-inch bubble, and fold them both down alongside the remaining length of balloon.

2. Join the bubbles with a locking twist.

3. Make a 7-inch bubble and fold it down alongside the remaining length of balloon.

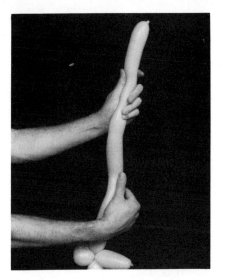

4. Join the 7-inch bubble to the remaining length of balloon with a locking twist at the point of your first locking twist.

5. This is what your snail looks like so far.

6. Squeeze the remaining length of balloon so that if fills up with air all the way to the tail. This will also lessen the tension in the tail section and allow you to proceed.

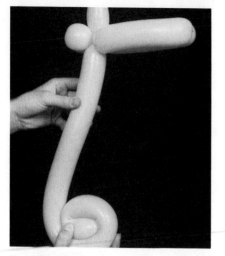

7. Starting from the tail end, roll the balloon up tightly in a coil.

8. Roll it all the way, until you run out of balloon.

9. Gently spread the two 7-inch bubbles apart with one hand. Place the bottom of the coil between the two 7-inch bubbles.

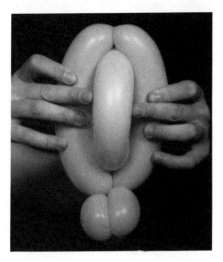

10. Gently roll the two 7-inch bubbles back over the coiled-up balloon until the coil is firmly wedged between the two 7-inch bubbles and stays in place.

11. Twist the 3-inch and 1-inch bubbles around together one-half turn. This is the completed snail.

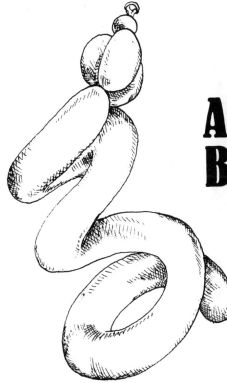

ADVANCED
BALLOON ANIMALS

PENGUIN

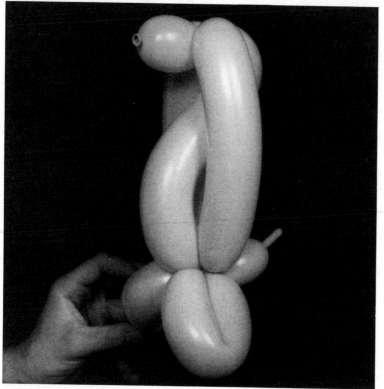

The original tuxedo! This one looks great when made with a white or black balloon.

 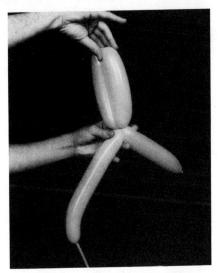 

1. Inflate a balloon, leaving a 4-inch tail on the end, and tie a knot. Make an 8-inch bubble, then a 6-inch bubble, and fold both bubbles down alongside the remaining length of balloon.

2. Join them with a locking twist.

3. Make a twist directly in the middle of the remaining length of balloon. Hold on to this twist so that it doesn't untwist.

4. Fold the first bubble formed by this twist in half so that the twists at each end of it are lined up next to each other.

5. Twist this folded bubble around on its ends a couple of times until it locks.

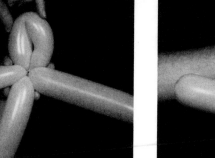

6. Now make a 1-inch bubble on the very tail end of the remaining bubble.

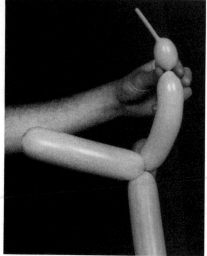

  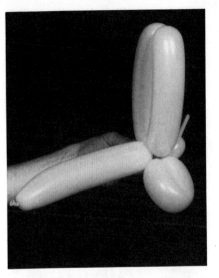

7. Fold the inside bubble (not the 1-inch bubble!) in half, as you did for the last bubble.

8. Twist the folded bubble around on its ends a couple of times until it locks, leaving the 1-inch bubble outside the twist.

9. You have just made the two flipperlike feet. This is what your penguin looks like so far.

the knot, through the
two 6-inch bubbles.
Don't push the entire
7-inch bubble through;
just that one little part
about 2 inches below
the knot.

10. Now gently spread the
two 6-inch bubbles
apart and lay the 7-
inch bubble between
them.

11. While spreading the
two 6-inch bubbles
apart with your fingers,
push the 7-inch bubble,
about 2 inches below

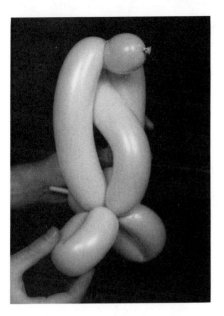 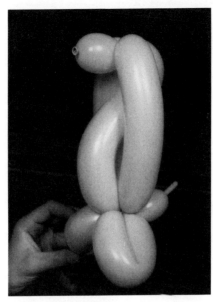

12. The rest of the 7-inch bubble will form the penguin's nose and slightly protruding belly. Adjust the nose and belly as pictured.

13. This is the completed penguin.

93

LION/CAT

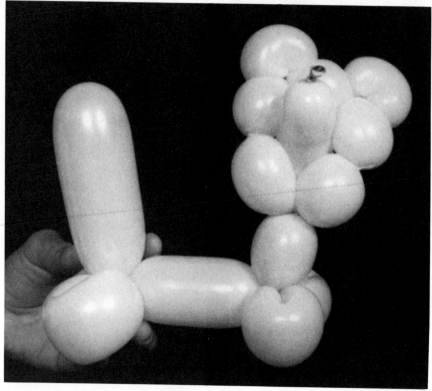

The king of balloon beasts!
Try the lion first, then its
domestic cousin. Everybody
I've ever given the cat to has
purred with joy. It is similar
to the lion, but a little bit
harder to make because you
have to hold on to a chain
of large and small bubbles.
It's well worth the time
required to perfect.

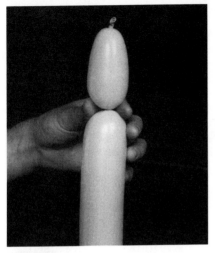

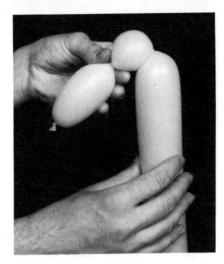

LION

1. Inflate a balloon, leaving a 5-inch tail on the end, and tie a knot. Make a 2-inch bubble for the nose.

2. You will now make seven 1-inch bubbles in a row. Remember to twist all small bubbles a few extra times. Begin by making the first 1-inch bubble.

3. Continue making the seven 1-inch bubbles, twisting each one in a different direction from the last. Be sure to hold on to all of the bubbles as you make them. They won't stay by themselves.

4. Line up the twist after the last 1-inch bubble and the twist between the 2-inch bubble and the first 1-inch bubble.

5. Join here with a locking twist, taking care not to let the 1-inch bubbles untwist. This is what you have so far.

6. To create the ears you will make an interesting twist with the third and fifth 1-inch bubbles. Pull the third 1-inch bubble out from the others.

7. Now pinch it with one hand and twist it around on its ends. Twist it all the way around a couple of times. The balloon will feel quite tight, like it's ready to pop, but with a gentle touch you should be able to get it around. You'll notice that the ears now have a pointed shape.

8. Repeat steps 6–7 with the fifth 1-inch bubble, twisting it around on its ends a couple of times. This is what the lion's head looks like so far.

9. Now take the 2-inch bubble that has the knot, fold it in half, and push the tip of the knot end through the ring of 1-inch bubbles you just made. Roll the ring of 1-inch bubbles around the 2-inch bubble until the 2-inch bubble is halfway through the ring.

10. Make a 2-inch bubble for the neck and hold on to it.

11. Make another 2-inch bubble and fold it in half.

12. Twist it around on its ends so that it locks.

13. This is what a balloon lion's front leg looks like.

14. Repeat this last twist with another 2-inch bubble for the other front leg: make a 2-inch bubble, fold it over, and twist it around on its ends. Now you have formed both of the lion's front legs.

15. Make a 3-inch bubble for the body and a 2-inch bubble for one of the back legs.

 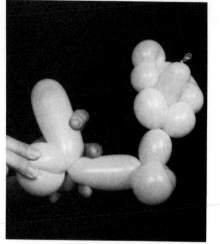 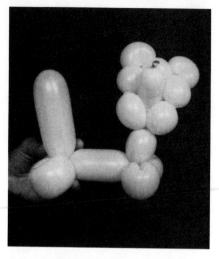

16. Fold the 2-inch bubble in half, just as you did for the lion's front legs, and twist it around on its ends.

17. Do the same thing for the second back leg: make one last 2-inch bubble, fold it in half, and twist it around on its ends. Be sure to leave a 3- or 4-inch bubble on the very end for a tail.

18. Spread your lion's legs and position him lying down, like the lion in the photo. This is the completed lion.

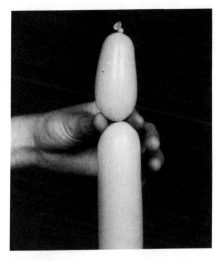

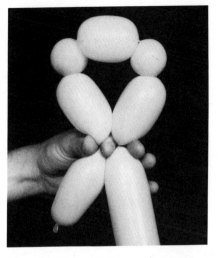

CAT

1. Inflate a balloon, leaving a 6-inch tail on the end, and tie a knot. Make a 3-inch bubble for the nose. Follow this with another 3-inch bubble, then a 1-inch bubble, a 3-inch bubble, and a 1-inch bubble.

2. Make one last 3-inch bubble. Hold bubbles so they don't untwist. Remember, make a few extra twists on the small bubbles and alternate twisting directions (away from you, toward you, away from you . . .).

3. Fold all of these bubbles over so that the last twist you made meets the twist behind the first 3-inch bubble.

101

4. Join here with a locking twist. Twist the loop formed by the 3-inch and 1-inch bubbles around a couple of times. This locks the head structure in place.

5. This is what the cat's head looks like so far.

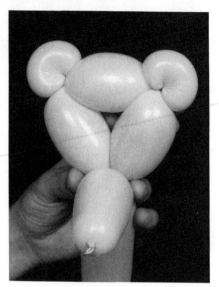

6. Using one of the 1-inch bubbles, follow steps 6–8 for the lion. Make the other ear with the remaining 1-inch bubble. This is what both of the cat's ears look like.

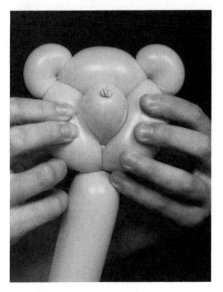

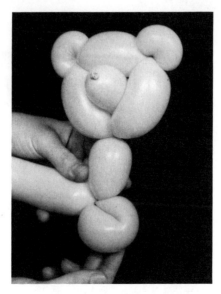

7. Now use the first 3-inch bubble to make the nose, as in steps 11–12 for the lion.

8. Following steps 13–15, make the cat's neck and a front paw. This is what the paw looks like.

9. Repeat with another 2-inch bubble. This is what both of the cat's front paws look like.

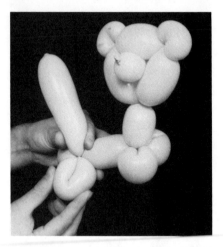  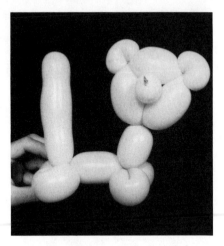

10. Now complete steps 18–20 for the lion to make the cat's body and back paws.

11. Straighten the last long length of balloon, the cat's tail, so that it is pointing up. Adjust the little paws so that the cat is lying down.

12. This is the completed cat.

TOUCAN

This one's a very exotic bird. It looks best if you use a brightly colored balloon.

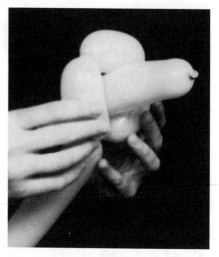

1. Inflate a balloon, leaving a 4-inch tail on the end, and tie a knot. Make a 5-inch bubble for the beak and three 3-inch bubbles for the head. Fold the three 3-inch bubbles over so that they form a triangle.

2. Twist all three 3-inch bubbles around a couple of times until the triangle locks in place.

3. Fold the 5-inch bubble in half and stick the knot end back through the triangle formed by the three 3-inch bubbles. Roll the triangle of 3-inch bubbles back around the 5-inch bubble until the 5-inch bubble is three-quarters of the way through the triangle.

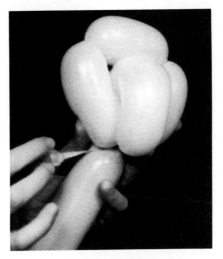

4. Wrap the knot around the twist at the base of the triangle a couple of times until it locks.

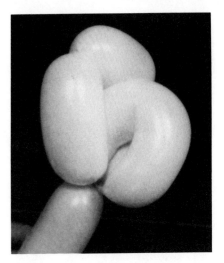

5. This is what the toucan's head looks like.

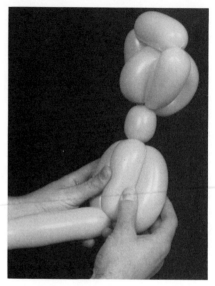

6. Make a 1-inch bubble for the neck and a 4-inch bubble for the body. Fold both bubbles down alongside the remaining length of balloon.

7. Make a locking twist at the point between the 1-inch and 4-inch bubbles.

8. Make another 4-inch bubble and gently spread the first two 4-inch

bubbles apart. Roll the first two 4-inch bubbles around the third 4-inch bubble until the third 4-inch bubble is all the way through them.

  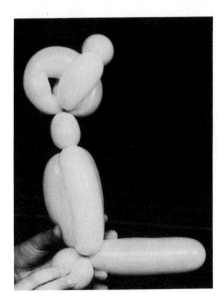

9. This locks the last 4-inch bubble. This is what your toucan looks like so far.

10. Make two 1-inch bubbles and fold them over next to each other.

11. Twist the 1-inch bubbles around each other a couple of times until they lock in place.

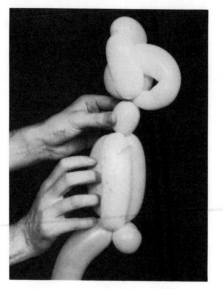

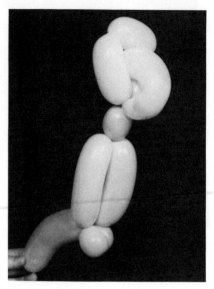

12. Curve the tail of your toucan slightly. Squeeze the tail until the whole tail fills up with air.

13. Position the toucan's head so that the long beak points forward and the body bubbles form two folded wings (on the side) and a rounded back.

14. This is the completed toucan.

FRENCH POODLE

This balloon animal is very fancy and impressive.

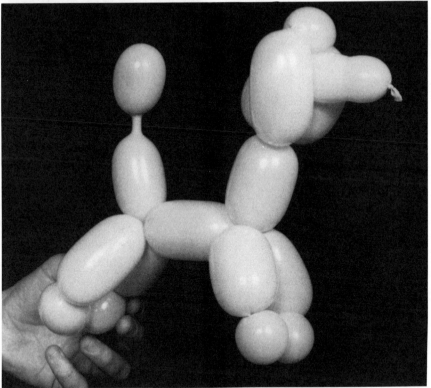

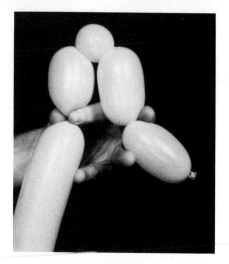  

1. Inflate a balloon, leaving a 5-inch tail on the end, and tie a knot. Make two 3-inch bubbles, a 1-inch bubble, and a third 3-inch bubble. Remember to twist them in opposite directions and hold on to the bubbles so they don't untwist.

2. Fold the last 3-inch bubble over until the twist at the back of the last 3-inch bubble meets the twist between the first and second 3-inch bubbles.

3. Twist the second and third 3-inch bubbles around each other a couple of times to lock the entire head structure in place.

112

4. Make another 3-inch bubble below the head. Hold on to it so that it doesn't untwist.

5. Follow this with a 3-inch bubble, then two 1-inch bubbles and another 3-inch bubble. Don't forget to make a couple of extra twists for the smaller bubbles. Hold on to these bubbles so that they don't untwist.

6. Fold all of these bubbles at the point between the two 1-inch bubbles. Line up the twist behind the last 3-inch bubble with the twist between the first two 3-inch bubbles.

7. Join here with a locking twist to secure the front legs of your French poodle.

8. Make a 3-inch bubble behind the front legs. Then another 3-inch bubble, two 1-inch bubbles, and a third 3-inch bubble. Leave 2 or 3 inches for the tail. Hold the bubbles so they don't untwist.

9. Fold all of these bubbles at the point between the two 1-inch bubbles. Again, line up the twist behind the last of these 3-inch bubbles with the twist between the first and second 3-inch bubbles. Join here with a locking twist.

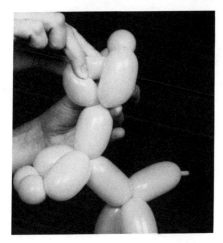 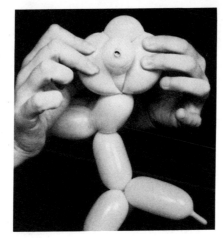 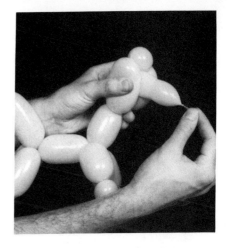

10. Return to the first 3-inch bubble, which has the knot. Fold it in half and begin to push the knot back between the ears of your French poodle.

11. Gently roll the ears around the nose.

12. Push the nose about halfway through the ears. Give a gentle tug on the knot to release a little extra balloon at the very tip while you squeeze the ears lightly at the same time.

13. Take the very tip of the tail of the balloon and stretch it quite a bit.

14. With both of your hands, squeeze the 3-inch bubble at the tail end of the balloon until a little bubble pops up at the very tip.

15. Adjust the various parts of your balloon and you have completed the French poodle.

BAT

With all of the excitement surrounding the revival of Batman, I thought that a balloon bat might be particularly appropriate. Whether the bat fanatics in your life are into comic book heroes or scary movies, their sonar will sizzle for this balloon bat. When October rolls around, make a bunch for Halloween.

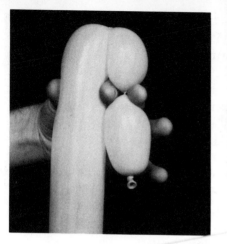 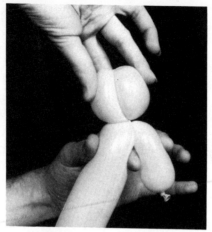 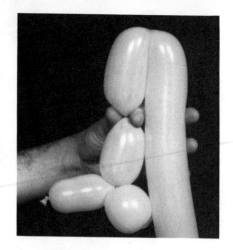

1. Inflate a balloon, leaving a 5-inch tail on the end, and tie a knot. Make a 2-inch bubble for the nose and a 1½-inch bubble for one of the bat's ears. Fold both of these bubbles down alongside the remaining length of balloon.

2. Join the bubbles with a locking twist.

3. Make a 2-inch bubble for the neck, then a 3-inch bubble, and fold both bubbles down alongside the remaining length of balloon.

 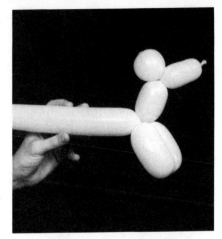 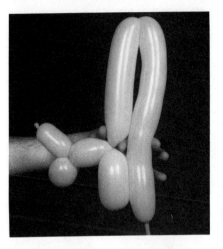

4. Join these bubbles with a locking twist.

5. This is what the bat looks like so far.

6. Make a 6-inch bubble and fold the remaining length of balloon down next to it.

  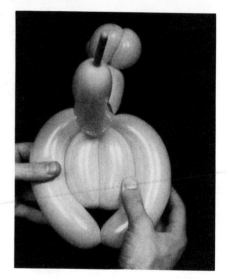

7. Pinch the remaining length of balloon where it meets the top of the 6-inch bubble. Twist the two 6-inch bubbles around each other a couple of times to lock them in place.

8. Gently spread the two 6-inch bubbles apart with your fingers. Roll them around the two 3-inch bubbles so that the 3-inch bubbles are surrounded by the 6-inch bubbles. Make

sure the 3-inch bubbles are facing front (see photo). The bubbles will be a bit snug, but they will fit.

9. Above is what your bat looks like from the back.

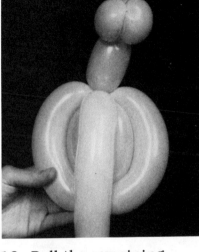

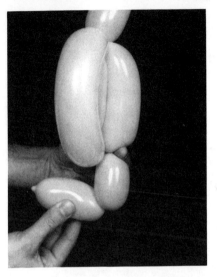

10. Pull the remaining length of balloon down the back of your bat.

11. Pinch the remaining length of balloon where it meets the twist at the bottom of your bat.

12. Form one little bubble with the little length of balloon that's left and fold the remaining length of balloon over.

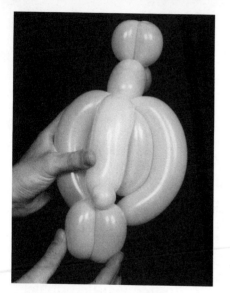

of the balloon. Twist these two little bubbles around each other a couple of times until they lock.

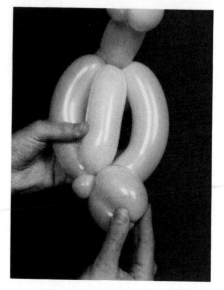

13. Pinch off a second bubble at the point where the remaining length meets the bottom of the bat. Be sure to leave a tiny bubble on the very end

14. Take both of these bubbles and wrap them around the twist at the base of your bat. You will actually push them through the 6-inch bubbles to do this. The

3-inch bubbles might pop out of the 6-inch bubbles. It's okay if they do. You will put them back later.

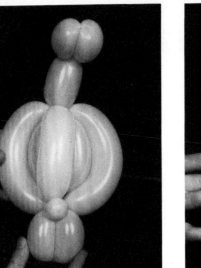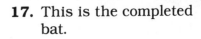

15. Position the two little bubbles at the base of your bat. They will now stay in place.

16. Replace the 3-inch bubbles inside the 6-inch bubbles if you need to. Remember to roll the 6-inch bubbles around the 3-inch bubbles.

17. This is the completed bat.

COBRA

You'll need the help of a friend for this one, but it's definitely worth the extra effort!

1. Inflate a balloon all the way to the end. Let all of the air out. Inflate the balloon a second time and let all of the air out again. The balloon should look very stretched out now.

2. With your thumb, hold the tail end of the balloon just above the base of your index finger. Let the rest of the balloon dangle down toward the floor.

3. Begin wrapping the balloon loosely around both your index and middle fingers. First wrap under your middle finger . . .

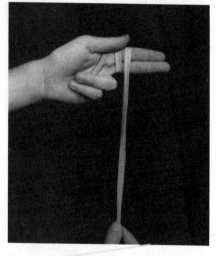 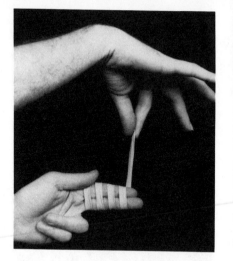 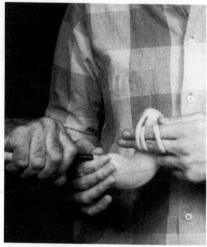

4. . . . and then over your index finger. Be careful not to wrap the balloon too tightly.

5. Continue wrapping until you have run out of balloon.

6. Have a friend insert the nozzle of the pump into the neck of the balloon while you continue holding the wrapped balloon around your fingers. Have your friend inflate the balloon. Be sure to hang on to the uninflated part so it coils as it is blown up. As it coils, it may slide off your fingers.

7. Inflate the balloon until you have a 1-inch tail on the very end. The rest of the balloon will be coiled up.

8. Slide your fingers out of the center of the coiled balloon if it hasn't already begun to slide off your fingers. Tie a knot. Squeeze the balloon well just below the knot to lessen the tension in the balloon.

9. Make a 2-inch bubble, then a 1½-inch bubble, and fold both bubbles down alongside the coiled length of the cobra.

10. Join the bubbles with a locking twist.

11. Give a gentle tug on the knot of the 2-inch bubble to release a little extra tension at the tip. Gently squeeze the 2-inch bubble while you tug on the knot.

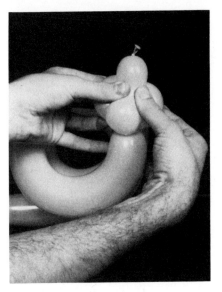

maneuver may take some practice; it's the hardest one in the book. But when you get it right, your cobra's head will give your creation a truly charmed appearance. You have now formed the head of the cobra.

12. Push the middle of the 2-inch bubble between the two 1½-inch bubbles.

13. Roll the two 1½-inch bubbles around the 2-inch bubble. Make sure the tip of the knot section sticks out over the two 1½-inch bubbles. This

129

14. This is the completed
cobra.

A FEW LAST WORDS

I hope you have enjoyed learning to make this new balloon menagerie. The scene on the cover of this book is just one idea for something to do with these animals once you've created them. With a little imagination and a few household items you can create your own scenes—from a Noah's ark scenario to your own balloon jungle. You can even try inventing your own imaginary animals.

If you need more balloons or pumps, there are mail-order sources on the next page. And if you're hooked on these little critters, be sure to look for my first book, *Balloon Animals*, which has 20 different animals, from a horse to a teddy bear.

Enjoy. I hope you make many people, including yourself, very happy.

MAIL-ORDER SOURCES

If you are unable to find balloons or pumps at your local novelty, joke, or magic shop, try one of these mail-order sources. All balloons are $15.00 a bag, postage and handling included, and come packaged 144 balloons to a bag. They are the highest-quality premium balloons available. All pumps are $6.00 each, postage and handling included. Please use U.S. currency on all orders and include an additional $3.00 postage on all orders going outside the United States.

Balloon Animals*
P.O. Box 711
Medford, MA 02155

Balloonology*
P.O. Box 301
Cambridge, MA 02238

*Massachusetts residents add 5 percent sales tax (75¢ per bag, 30¢ per pump).